THE LIBRARY OF THE
PLANETS™

EARTH
Luke Thompson

The Rosen Publishing Group's
PowerKids Press™
New York

For the St. Andrew's Library

Published in 2001 by The Rosen Publishing Group, Inc.
29 East 21st Street, New York, NY 10010

First Edition

Book Design: Michael Caroleo and Michael de Guzman

Photo Credits: Cover image and pp. 6, 12 (bottom), 15, 16 (continents), 19, 22 Photodisc; pp. 4, 7, 8 (Illustrations) by Michael Caroleo; p.11 (Illustration) by Maria Melendez; p .20 (spring, summer, fall) © Photri; pp. 12 (winter 1/4) © William A. Bake/CORBIS; p.16 (mountains) © Janez Skok/CORBIS; p.16 (grasslands) © Kevin R. Morris/Corbis; p.12 (Pacific Ocean) © Joel W. Rogers/CORBIS.

Thompson, Luke
        Earth / by Luke Thompson.
            p. cm.–(The library of the planets)
        Includes index.
        Summary: Examines the planet Earth, including its geology, atmosphere, climate, seasons,
        moon, and its place in the solar system and the universe.
        ISBN 0-8239-5644-X (alk. paper)
        1. Earth–Juvenile literature. [1. Earth.] I. Title. II. Series.

    QB631.4 .T46 2000
    525–dc21   00-024770

Manufactured in the United States of America

Contents

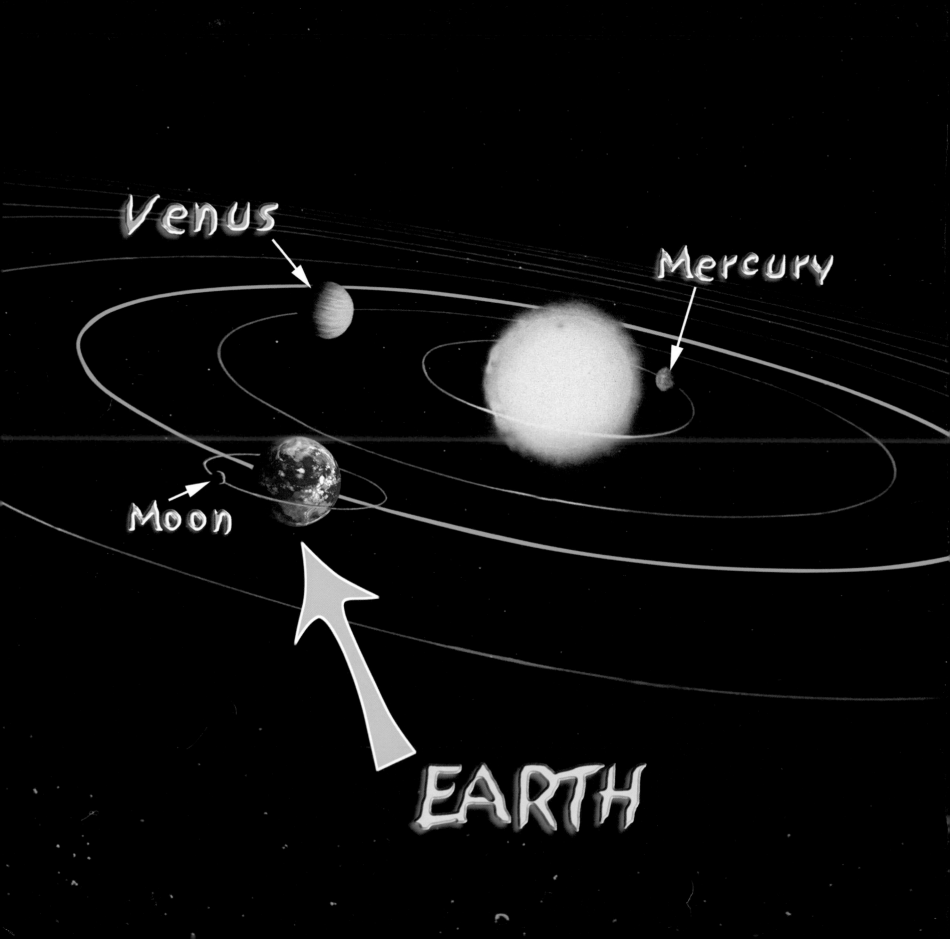

How Earth Orbits the Sun

Earth is one of the nine planets in our **solar system**. A solar system is a group of planets that travels around a single star. When planets travel around a star, we say that they **orbit** that star. In our solar system, the star that the nine planets orbit is the Sun. We measure the length of a year on a planet by how long it takes that planet to orbit the Sun. It takes Earth 365 days to orbit the Sun. This is why we say that a year on Earth is 365 days long. Earth travels around the Sun very fast, at about 67,000 miles (107,826 km) per hour.

It is the Sun's **gravity** that stops Earth and all the other planets from floating off into space. Gravity is the pull between two objects. The bigger an object is, the stronger it pulls on other objects. The Sun is the biggest object in our solar system. It has the strongest gravitational pull. That is why it is the center of the solar system.

Earth is the third planet from the Sun. Also pictured are Mercury and Venus, the first and second planets from the Sun.

Earth's Rotation

Earth orbits the Sun. Earth also **rotates**, which means that it spins around. All nine planets rotate. Earth rotates once every 24 hours. It is this spinning around that causes night and day. When a certain side of Earth is facing the Sun, it is daytime on that side. Then Earth rotates, and that side turns away from the Sun. This is when it becomes night on Earth.

Earth rotates on an **axis**. The axis is an imaginary pole that runs through the center of the planet. Imagine taking an orange and sticking a pencil straight through the center. The pencil is like Earth's axis. The tip of the pencil and the eraser would be like the North and South Poles.

Earth rotates once every 24 hours. It is this rotation that causes night and day. Earth revolves around the Sun in 365 days.

Mantle

Core

Crust

The Crust, Mantle, and Core

Earth is made up of three different layers. These three layers are called the **crust**, the **mantle**, and the **core**. The crust is the thinnest layer. It is the outer layer of rock and soil that covers all of Earth. The crust of Earth is always changing. When the ground shakes during an earthquake, the planet's crust changes. It also changes when a volcano **erupts**.

Underneath the crust lies a very thick layer of rock called the mantle. The mantle is almost 1,900 miles (3,000 km) thick. The mantle of Earth is made up of a mixture of rock and **magma**. Magma is hot liquid rock.

Underneath the mantle is the core. The core is the very center of Earth. At the core, the temperature gets hotter than the surface of the Sun. The outer part of the core is made of liquid metal. The inner part is made of solid metal, probably iron. In total, Earth is made up of about 34 percent iron.

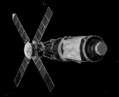

Earth is separated into three parts called the crust, mantle, and core. The outer part of the core is made of hot liquid metal that is about 7,400 degrees Fahrenheit (4,100 degrees C).

Earth's Atmosphere

The **atmosphere** of a planet is the layer of air that surrounds it. Earth's atmosphere is made of several different kinds of **gases**. A gas is something that is not a solid or a liquid. It has no exact shape.

Earth's atmosphere is made up mostly of two kinds of gases. The most common gas in the air is nitrogen. The second most common gas is oxygen. There are also small amounts of water, dust, ice, and salt in Earth's air. Earth's atmosphere acts as a kind of blanket to keep the world warm at night. It stops much of the heat from escaping into space. The atmosphere also screens out harmful rays from the Sun.

Earth's atmosphere is made up of many different layers. The bottom layer, where clouds form and planes fly, is called the troposphere. Next is the stratosphere, which rises to about 50 miles (80 km) above Earth's surface. At the top of the stratosphere is a layer of ozone. Ozone is a heavy form of oxygen that protects Earth from the Sun's rays.

The Living Planet

Scientists believe that Earth is the only planet in our solar system where living things can survive. They believe that this is true because of Earth's air, water, and temperature. These three elements create the conditions that all living things need to survive.

The air in Earth's atmosphere is necessary for all living things. Oxygen is very important. We could not live if there wasn't oxygen in the air for us to breathe.

The temperature on Earth is good for plant and animal life. Temperatures on Earth are not as cold or hot as they are on the other planets in our solar system. It is rarely too hot or too cold for things to survive on Earth.

Living things also need water. Fresh water is needed for drinking, washing, and farming. Earth is the only planet in our solar system with a large reserve of water.

This is a view of Earth from the Moon. In the background is a separate image of the Pacific Ocean, the largest ocean in the world.

The Blue Planet

Seventy-one percent of Earth's surface is covered with water. Earth is sometimes called the Blue Planet. From outer space, the water covering Earth makes it look blue. Two kinds of water cover Earth's crust. Most of this water is salt water. The other kind of water is fresh water.

The biggest bodies of water on Earth are called oceans. They are filled with salt water. The four oceans on Earth are the Atlantic, the Pacific, the Arctic, and the Indian Ocean. A sea is smaller than an ocean and is also made up of salt water. Lakes are large bodies of water. A lake is different from a sea because it is completely surrounded by land. Most lakes are made of fresh water. Some lakes are as big as a sea.

Rivers are snakelike trails of moving water. Rivers are an important part of Earth's water system because they carry water from one place to another.

Earth is 71 percent water, which is why it is called the Blue Planet. Shown here are the Atlantic, Pacific, and Arctic Oceans.

There are seven **continents** on Earth. The continents are Asia, Europe, North America, South America, Africa, Australia, and Antarctica.

The continents are made up of different types of **terrain**. Terrain is the kind of land in a certain region. Some kinds of terrain are good for living things. Other kinds of terrain make life difficult for plants and animals.

Grassland is one kind of terrain found on Earth. It is easy for people to live on this kind of terrain. They can farm and raise animals for food. Mountains are another type of terrain. Mountains are large hills that rise out of Earth's surface. Every continent has some kind of mountainous terrain.

Desert is a type of terrain made mostly out of sand. It is hard to live in the desert. Plants do not grow well there because there is not much water. The worst kind of terrain to live in is found on the continent of Antarctica. Antarctica is covered with snow and ice.

There are many different types of terrain, such as grasslands and mountains, on Earth's seven continents.

The Moon

A moon is a large, round object that orbits a planet. Moons circle planets the same way that planets circle the Sun. Some planets have several moons, but Earth has only one. Earth's moon is one quarter the size of the planet. At night when the Sun is down, the Moon is bright. The Moon does not give off its own light. It reflects light from the Sun. As the Moon orbits the Earth, we see different parts of it lit up. The Sun shines on one side of the Moon at a time. There is a light side and a dark side of the Moon. These sides affect the **phases** of the Moon. The phases of the Moon help explain how the Moon looks from Earth. When the light side of the Moon is facing directly toward Earth, it is called a full Moon. When the dark side is turned toward Earth, it is called a new Moon. A half Moon occurs when half of the light side and half of the dark side of the Moon are facing Earth.

This picture shows a full, half, quarter, and crescent moon.

Full Moon

Half Moon

Crescent Moon

Quarter Moon

Four Seasons

There are four different seasons on Earth. The seasons change as Earth orbits the Sun. A year on Earth is made up of one spring, one summer, one fall, and one winter. When a year has passed, the seasons start over again. They always come in the same order.

Summer is the warmest of the four seasons. In the summertime, plants and animals get a lot of the Sun's energy. Winter is the coldest season. In some places, it snows in the winter. Spring is the season when winter changes into summer. In the spring, the snow in cold places melts, and the weather turns warmer. Trees and flowers begin to bloom. Fall is the season when summer changes into winter. The warm days slowly get colder. In the fall, the leaves begin to change color and fall from the trees.

Fall, winter, spring, and summer make up the four seasons on Earth. When the Sun shines most directly on the Northern Hemisphere of Earth, it is called the summer solstice. When the Sun shines most directly on the Southern Hemisphere, it is called the winter solstice.

Earth and the Universe

Scientists are always trying to learn more about our planet. On February 11, 2000, the **space shuttle** *Endeavor* headed for outer space. **Astronauts** on board the *Endeavor* spent 11 days using **radar** signals to make detailed maps of the Earth's surface. The radar system received information on more than 47.6 million square miles (123,283,434 sq km) of the Earth's surface. It is also important to learn about the way things work beyond Earth. One day we may want to try living on a different planet. Before we can do that, we need to learn about the planets around us. The solar system we live in is part of a **galaxy**. A galaxy is made of several billion stars packed closely together. Our Sun belongs to a galaxy called the **Milky Way**. The Milky Way is just one of the many galaxies in our **universe**. The universe is huge, and planet Earth is just a small part of it.

Glossary

astronauts (AS-troh-notz) Members of a crew on a spacecraft.

atmosphere (AT-muh-sfeer) The layer of gases that surrounds an object in space. On Earth, this layer is air.

axis (AK-sis) A straight line on which an object turns or seems to turn.

continents (KON-tin-entz) The seven great masses of land on Earth.

core (KOR) The center layer of a planet.

crust (KRUST) The outer layer of a planet.

erupts (ih-RUPTS) When something bursts out of something else.

galaxy (GAH-lik-see) A large group of stars and the planets that circle them.

gases (GAS) Substances that are not liquid or solid, have no size or shape of their own, and can increase without limit.

grassland (GRAS-land) Farmland made up mostly of grass.

gravity (GRAH-vih-tee) The natural force that causes objects to move or tend to move toward the center of Earth.

magma (MAG-muh) A hot, liquid rock beneath Earth's surface.

mantle (MAN-tul) The middle layer of Earth that lies between the core and the crust of Earth's surface.

Milky Way (MIL-kee WAY) The galaxy that contains our Sun and solar system.

orbit (OR-bit) When a planet circles around another object.

phases (FAY-zez) The different stages of the Moon as seen from Earth.

radar (RAY-dar) An instrument for determining the distance, direction, and speed of unseen objects by using radio waves.

rotates (ROH-taytz) When something moves in a circle.

solar system (SOH-ler SIS-tem) A group of planets that circles a star. Our solar system has nine planets, which circle the Sun.

space shuttle (SPAYS SHUT-uhl) A reusable spacecraft meant to carry people and machinery between Earth and space.

terrain (TUH-rayn) An area of land.

universe (YOO-nih-vers) Everything that is around us.

Index

A
astronauts, 22
atmosphere, 10, 13
axis, 6

C
continents, 17
core, 9
crust, 9, 14

E
Endeavor, 22

G
galaxy, 22
gases, 10
gravity, 5

M
mantle, 9
Milky Way, 22
Moon, 18

P
phases, 18

S
seasons, 21
solar system, 5, 13, 22
space shuttle, 22
Sun, 5, 6, 9, 10, 18, 21, 22

T
temperature, 9, 13
terrain, 17

W
water, 13, 14, 17

If you want to learn more about Earth and the other planets, check out these Web sites:
http://msgc.engin.umich.edu
http://spaceart.com